Runway to Lucky Leadership

Pradeep Gowda

Copyright © 2023 Pradeep Gowda

All rights reserved.

ISBN: 9798374093056

DEDICATION

To my experiences and learnings!

CONTENTS

	Preface	vii
1	All or Nothing	1
2	The Greatest Power of All	6
3	Common Sense ain't Cheap	11
4	Take me to your Leader	16
5	No-Nonsense Leader	20
6	How to manage Perceptions	25
7	What should you want in your manager	29
8	Are you working for a Brand	33
9	Halo effect and Leadership Crisis	42
10	Lessons from Leaders	46

PREFACE

I have come to believe that a leader becomes lucky or gains luck by following a series of steps and acquires a multitude of traits that is outlined in this book.

The attempt here is to reflect on the fundamentals, the very basics that are needed to deliver the given job, while keeping things simple.

This is an outcome of my experiences from various phases of my professional life.

The content in this book primarily comes from the collection of articles that I wrote and published on Linkedin (removed now) between 2014 to 2016. There are changes though (some subtle and some significant additions) in all chapters.

In many a way, I would say this book is kinda monologue and a note to self!

It's a light read. I hope you will relate to some of the content.

I welcome your views and thank you for your time!

This book wouldn't have materialized without the support of my wife – Kavya and my daughter – SiRii. They are my pillars of strength and encouragement!

1 ALL OR NOTHING!

With so much material available nowadays (at a click of a button) on success, leadership, the many to-do's, the know-how's, the habits of successful people etc. etc., It's very hard to decode the true recipe to reach there (. i.e., your goal, your destination...)

Taking in all that is out there, I firmly believe it just boils down to the simple motto: "All or Nothing".

How badly do you want 'what you want'?

    Do you have a choice?

What are you willing to risk to get there?

Are you concerned about the opportunity cost (knowing that's a bummer)?

Are you crystal clear about your "want" ('chiseled on rock' type of clarity)? Can you foresee & visualize it? Dream about it?

Do you see the bigger picture? Are you able to see the forest before counting the trees?

Do you know whom do you want to sing to? .... your target audience?

Have you figured out your true Strengths and Weaknesses?

Do you know how to play to your strengths & work-around your weaknesses?

Answers to the above would no-doubt lead you to a <u>far better</u> place in your quest to reach your goals.

Many mis-directional attempts **without** much of a hunger to achieve, and lack of vision' is a classic case of many failed stories.

Recognizing what went wrong and pivoting back to the path of mission wouldn't materialize without reflecting on the fundamentals listed above.

This chapter in its earlier version carried the

heading "Clarity + Higher Purpose = A Recipe for Success" (a bit cheesy ah!)

Nevertheless, was hoping to drive home the point, only to realize that the title wasn't apt. So, now it is "ALL or NOTHING" and here's the reason why it is called so:

1. When we have a choice, we do **not** give our very best, but without a choice all of us have the potential to switch on our animal instinct to get what we want and to go where we want to. People get more creative when everything is at stake. Innovations and Discoveries happen around this phase.

2. Having a choice derails & destroys the **urge** to get above the crowd because by nature we are programmed to take the easy way out, but only a few take the high road and get there, and those are who we look up to as role-models.

3. Take the present-day scenario or history, it is filled with people with grit, gusto, and determination who we read about, idolize, and make movies on.

Nobody had it easy and if anybody had it so, it is nothing but a moment of glory and a facade to say the most.

As per me, Larry Ellison of Oracle does complete

justice to this motto – All or Nothing. He comes from a difficult background, born to single parent from a lower middle-class community and adopted by his uncle & aunt, Ellison grew up in Lower East Side, Manhattan and South Side, Chicago. Worked as a programmer for many organizations for years in his early days after dropping out from college.

Partnering with Ed Oats (his former colleague) and Bob Miner (his mentor), Ellison went out to create and market 'Oracle – RDMS' in the 1980s. The company grew rapidly through ups and downs; and after several high-profile acquisitions like Siebel, Sun Microsystems, Peoplesoft etc., Ellison now commands a net worth of more than $60B and is counted among the top 10 wealthiest in the world per Bloomberg Billionaires Index.

It has been reported that Ellison owns about 98% of an Island in Hawaii too.

Now that's a prime example of somebody who gives enough credence to the motto – 'All or Nothing'. Ellison has gotten ALL or probably more than what he went for, I would assume.

When you go in, go in for the kill. Take it ALL. Be Unapologetic...

Runway to Lucky Leadership

2 THE GREATEST POWER OF ALL

I read this statement "The ***Power to Choose*** is the **Greatest Power of ALL**" just like many would have while browsing through the internet; and then without a second thought I completely dismissed this statement, as most of us would do.

Well, what is new in that statement and how is it even called 'POWER to Choose' because most of us have found ourselves without a choice, haven't we? Then, where is the POWER in it, at all? With all that is at stake – job, life, liking's etc. where is CHOICE here, except maybe the power to choose the type of Pizza, Ice-Cream flavor maybe, or Biriyani!

Well, my point is, do we have a choice at all? And

the answer to this ***teaser*** question is a **'resounding YES'**.

But, how?

Here's my **to-do's** to ensure that you get to 'ably and judiciously' utilize and apply the GREATEST POWER of ALL!

1. **Get to know your *true* Priorities**. The sooner, one realizes his/her real priorities, only then there could be a focused action to accomplish them, everything else is energy drain and pushing days. When you know your true priorities, you will know your goals, you will know your path (what to do and most importantly you will also get to know 'what not to do' that could hurt your priorities), eventually your chosen path will slowly show 'moments of truths (small victories)' which in-turn will provide the much-needed energy to get to your priorities.

2. **Focus on needs, not wants.** NOTE: this is relative to each – somebody's 'needs' could be another person's 'wants'. The differentiator here is to know that 'nugget' and ably tread accordingly. The definition of wants and needs changes as we grow in our lives, which is ok and is ideal (like they say, 'Greed is Good!' ever heard that? But the key is knowing when and where to stop. This is what counts for a life lived well.)

3. **Do not fret over things that are <u>not</u> directly in**

your control (Worrying is a waste of your intelligence - read this somewhere. Not my line!)

4. **Practice Realism.** Idealistic views and approaches are fine, but need to ensure <u>what works where</u> (this is key to all the challenges)

5. **Do not Subvert.** Take time, understand, learn the nuances, relate to people around, stakeholder management is key, it is not always what & how you view, but that view should match the upward purpose & opinion for your progress and success.

6. **Know and get a good handle on both - Vision and Mission**. Dream big (vision) but know the execution path (mission), without which it's nothing but a mere daydream (i.e., vision without action is a daydream) and it's a nightmare vice-versa (i.e., action without a vision.)

7. **Tune yourself to outcome-based activities**. Know the consequences. Do not act without thinking of the prospects. Envision the next steps. ***Why are you doing, what you are doing?*** It could be a simple email but know what you intended to achieve with your email.

8. It's commonly said that one should know 'what to do, what to say and when to say. I would suggest that it is more important that one should know 'what **not** to say and what **not** to do'. Simple things do add up!

No-doubt all the above pointers can be imbibed at any given point of time in one's life, but largely comes with experience. Experience is a great teacher only if we choose to learn from it.

The POWER to CHOOSE gives you a sense of authority and control, because it's on your terms. You are the author of your life in the truest sense, not merely pushed around by situations.

It is **REAL power**, but ***very few*** get to it. Whoever has exercised this and has ***attained the desired outcome***, has done so judiciously, wisely and with a ton of sacrifices. The key to a fulfilling life!

If you think back and think harder, it has always been a <u>choice,</u> but we all succumb to desires, flattery, the ill-pressures (peer, society, & self-expectations) and then we complain when life doesn't turn-out the way we want it, when we willingly have chosen the easy or the crowded route.

Jay Z (American Rapper and Music Producer) fits into this category where I feel (the little that I know through media) that he has ably applied this motto and has chosen his path in life and has gotten to where he is now.

Considering his growing-up years where he chose to sell drugs to make ends meet, to making & selling music; and then to creating his own label, he seems to have hit the right notes in his growth story and seemed to have willingly chosen his path.

The story goes that when record companies weren't interested in his first music album, he along with his buddies created their own label 'Roc-A-Fella' records and launched the album which became a success. That's gutsy with a whole lot of conviction.

Today, Jay Z is considered as the world's richest musician by net worth, and he became the first rapper to be inducted into Songwriters Hall of Fame'. In 2021 Jay Z was inducted into the 'Rock and Roll Hall of Fame.

Reading JayZ's life story makes one kinda believe that he might have in real terms used the Power to Choose to the best.

3 COMMON SENSE AIN'T CHEAP

One trait that is most important to unapologetic leadership is 'Common Sense'!

With this trait built-in or imbibed into our system, everything else takes care of itself – Conviction, Courage etc... etc.....

Common Sense, irrespective of its versatility, is rarely used in our day-to-day life, instead we look at every other ***trick*** to play with. Let me try and explain:

It's common sense to build 'trust' everywhere and with everyone. Now, how hard is it to know that we got to build "Trust" as we navigate through life.

> Trust is the basic quality that supersedes every other aspect (tangible or in-tangible.)
>
> Trust is 'fundamental', it's the ethos of living beings, it's the unwritten code to "survive", also most definitely to "thrive". Think about it, harder please!
>
> With trust, you can gain relationships, businesses, grow in a job, countries sign treaties based on trust (primarily), while the rest is paperwork and systemics to put in-place a mechanism to address the concern.
>
> Basically, trust is key for anything and everything.

So, why don't we realize that it's **'common sense'** to build trust, however most of us either ignore or attach far less significance than required.

> > Would you go out with a person who is untrustworthy?
> > Would you do business with unreliable folks?
> >
> > Would you want to work with folks who aren't dependable or treacherous?

> Would you believe in your kid/spouse/dear one, who has multiple times broken your trust? ....the answer is NO....why would you? ... of course and unless, the intention is to lead a miserable life.

We somehow lose sight of the fact that it's just *Common Sense* to build and retain 'Trust'.

Likewise, it's common sense to 'believe' in yourself.

> Self-belief and self-confidence will get you where you want to go instead of being pushed or thrown-at situations.
>
> With stronger confidence in self, you will have choices and you can exercise your freedom, creativity etc. In-short, you can lead a fulfilling life, now, who doesn't want that?
>
> Its common sense to 'treat' others on par. One cannot deny this fact.
>
> Its common sense to do the 'right thing' (legally, ethically, morally) in any set-up. No contest there!
>
> Its common sense to protect and preserve your 'health', else its costly to repair and replenish.

Its common sense to not 'cheat', else that truly would suck everything you may have, isn't it? again ties back to trust.

Its common sense to 'pay dues on-time', else you end-up paying fines (sometimes, those late fees could be deep and could require legal attention. Nobody wants that!)

Its common sense to 'follow the law'. We know that ain't cheap if broken.

Its common sense to see the forest before counting the trees – see the larger picture, get to the objective of the exercise instead of getting all muddled-up with just noise.
Never **not** know that 'Quality is Common Sense'. Imbibe it, adopt it, and adapt to it.

It's just common-sense to 'time' your communication and announcement to larger audience for better impact or to reduce unnecessary after-effects.

I can go on and on, but you get the point, I think.

Common Sense, like any other trait needs to be practiced & applied (diligently and religiously.) Requires discipline and dedication, and it doesn't come cheap.

Common Sense like Simplicity isn't easy!

4 TAKE ME TO YOUR LEADER

I can unequivocally say that there are 2 broad categories of leaders.

> one who holds a position of authority.

> and then, there are those who lead.

People follow those who lead because they inspire us, they elicit a sense of purpose and truly answer the 'why' (provide reasons, not excuses); whereas folks in positions of authority simply go-through the mechanics of the work involved and try to implement. They aren't followed nor believed, but simply reported to; and I am certain that folks reporting into them wouldn't think twice to de-link that chain if and when they get an opportunity.

I also feel that folks who lead (call it 'lucky leaders') ought to have the 6Cs:

1. Conviction
2. Courage
3. Compassion
4. Character
5. Coaching
6. Common Sense

(I have intentionally changed the order of conviction and courage, where conviction is shown first in the order because I strongly feel that without conviction there is no way anyone can be courageous for the entirety of a topic; everything else is a momentary burst of high, just to demonstrate toughness which would no-doubt fizzle out when debated based on facts.)

Conviction in self, in his/her team-members, in the process and more importantly conviction to effect changes and to stand by it.

Courage to handle tough discussions in an objective manner when there would be several occasions which may make you dither away or get swayed and lose focus. The courage to take tough decisions, stand-up for the team, and more importantly to take full responsibility and accountability.

Compassion is a vital ingredient that aids to fulfil leadership in entirety, not to be ignored. EQ can be traced to this trait in a leader.

Character defines the leader. It tells if the leader is a class-apart or without class! A leader who fishes in mundane aspects without relying on facts nor figures (read: numbers, metrics); is simply an outcast.

Coaching is one of the strongest traits of a true leader. A leader will no-doubt create more leaders (not just followers) by effective coaching and grooming. A leader identifies the problem statement, discusses solutions while applying preventive and corrective measures as needed.

Common Sense is another hallmark of a leader that cannot be ignored. We talked quite a bit in the earlier section on this trait.

Howard Schultz, to my mind, is an above-par leader who has demonstrated all these traits, by and large.

His conviction in Starbucks cannot go unnoticed when he came back after his initial stint to purchase the company from the founders in 1987 with the help other investors and had the courage to take

Starbucks overseas to Asia & Europe, while eventually growing a small coffee shop from the earlier 11 stores to 33000 in about 75 countries.

Remarkable is an understatement, when considering the ups and downs that Starbucks went through, particularly during the 2008 financial crisis.

Howard, the leader he is, rolled out landmark programs – a first in the retail Industry, where Starbucks provided comprehensive healthcare to both full-timers & part-timers, and stock options to employees.

He also instituted tuition free online educational program for the benefit of employees.

According to Forbes, in 2008 Schultz ordered that Starbucks stop selling melted-cheese breakfast sandwiches because the smell was masking the aroma of coffee, the company's core offering. Key leaders pushed back and argued for the sandwiches, and ultimately, they found a compromise. Now, Starbucks is once again selling them and cooking them in a way that makes them less aromatic.

Luigi Bonini, Starbucks' head of product development, told Forbes, "Howard can always be convinced."

That's my leader there!

5 NO-NONSENSE LEADER

The bigger question is, who is a no-nonsense leader?

Is he/she different than the other gamut of leaders out there?

Is there a small sub-set of leaders who can be categorized as no-nonsense types?

In the earlier section, we talked the key traits that any leader ought to have; and I referred it to as **6Cs**, in which one of them is 'Character'.

Now after re-thinking this ever-interesting topic, I have come to believe that all traits or none of the traits can be realized without a leader having a strong 'Character' and character it is what makes one stand-out from the rest and gets the deserving respect & admiration.

Most of you already know that not everybody gets '***deserving***' respect; and the less said on admiration the better it is, because admiring somebody for their leadership skills is a rarity and that's why we have a handful of 'true' leaders.

I got to use one of Bruce Lee's famous sayings which is just apt here "Knowledge will give you power, but character respect".

Re-purposing a snippet from the previous section: "Character defines the leader. It tells if the leader is a class-apart or without class. A so-called leader who fishes in mundane aspects without relying on facts nor figures; is simply an outcast."

I am not trying to say that a leader shouldn't be caring, approachable, logical, objective oriented, decisive, responsive etc., but simply put, I say that a no-nonsense leader ought to have '***character***' first to have all the rest of the attributes. Do you agree?

Re-casting one of the oft-repeated famous quotes, I would put it as "The true measure of a leader's character lies in the face of adversity and not in comfort and convenience". Like Abe Lincoln said

"Nearly all men can stand adversity, but if you want to test a man's character then give him power.'

Leaders need to go back to the basics and re-visit their deeds because character lies in the ***conduct*** and can be contagious!

I am quite certain that most of you perhaps by now have started to think who (basis your experience) was or is a no-nonsense leader. It is difficult to identify one among the lot, it is a nugget, isn't it?

If at all you can identify more than 2 with whom you have worked, then I would say you are fortunate; and you should continue to be associated with those leaders (probably become their mentee.) Never lose contact with those because there are life-lessons that you shouldn't miss, that no-doubt aids one's overall growth.

Luis Urzua is a classic example of a leader with character. He is in my view a no-nonsense leader who displayed exemplary bravado and most importantly gave utmost clarity & instilled hope to his team of 33 who were holed up 700 mts deep (more than 0.5 kms) below the ground in a mine.

I am referring to the Chilean mine accident of 2010 where 33 miners were trapped for 69 days (more than 2 months.)

Luis, the shift boss convinced the trapped miners to ration food until they were discovered by having each miner eat a tea-spoon of tuna and half a glass of milk on the same spot & same time for every 2 days to eliminate the idea of any cheating or misgiving, because it is easy to break-away and be on own, in situations as these.

He ensured that the miners had a task to deliver and kept them busy & focused on the single most objective of getting out while not losing mental strength and hope.

Some were assigned to dig for fresh water, some others were tasked to build a toilet, map out the tunnel to see other ways out, while one of them became a religious head. He made them simulate 'day and night' by shining lights and ensured healthy habits in unseeming situations.

Every act was to re-assure **hope** and re-emphasis the message that they will survive, while keeping the ***focus on how to help achieve that***.

This is no less than a miracle for a leader to demonstrate and deliver strong discipline, and patience given the impossible situation.

Finally, when it was time for miners to come out to cheering crowd one-by-one from the deep, Luis was the last one to come!

Luis' is a heart of gold!

Runway to Lucky Leadership

6 HOW TO MANAGE PERCEPTIONS?

People are perceptive by nature and they make decisions based on how they feel mostly, hence it is vital to ensure a better perception of yourself and how others see you.

10 Nuggets that Lucky Leaders follow to navigate life and to be successful!

1. Be Clear and have sensible conversations, *else* do not speak.

2. Highlight your achievements in the right forums. Summary of accomplishments is good enough, instead of repeatedly emphasizing. Do **not overdo it.**

3. Do **not** react, but only respond. Note that Response is data-driven, hence think and, think hard before responding.

4. Do not repeat again & again (no need to over communicate in meetings or discussions; smart ones will know what your role is and what your contribution is? And every group has a smart one who will eventually play a big role. So, practice **patience. It's a virtue.**)

5. Be creative (***visualize the next steps*** and act on it.)

6. Ensure that you are clear on the **vision** and tread accordingly!

7. Speak-up and speak **eloquently**; and **articulate** better (not abstract, but *substance*)

8. Go back to the basics when working on an activity.

    Answers to the questions to help your path – what is driving the need? why? how and when? Laying out the ***fundamentals*** and **keeping them simple** always helps.

9. Promise Less, but ***Deliver More***

10. And ***lastly***, Lunch-table or Coffee room discussion topics: A strict no-no to all contentious issues, such as politics, religion, ethnicity related, cultural perspectives etc. Always prone to conflict. Avoid it completely. Wouldn't aid your growth.

How to change perceptions?'

In a recent conversation with one of my well-wishers, I think I found an answer which I truly believe can be applied and pursued to re-gain or ensure a better perception.

I was told that perception can be changed by sending out proper signals at proper intervals which should emphasize what you want to communicate that could potentially negate the earlier impression about you. Follow the 10 nuggets to help further.

The *idea* is to ensure that you as a person take control & full responsibility to change the earlier perception.

7 WHAT SHOULD YOU WANT IN YOUR MANAGER?

Here's a list of 5 **minimums** that is expected from any Manager (maybe not a leader, but the one you report into.)

1. Should possess **Reasonable** Listening Ability and Empathy.

2. Weighs the pros and cons; and takes positions on an 'objective' basis on **most occasions** rather than getting carried-away with subjectivity.

3. **Fair** weightage to 'one & all' in the team, because any 'small or large group' is bound to have favoritism that no-doubt takes away the level

playing field (which is deliberate at times to override the competition.)

4. **Responsiveness**. Being Responsive' is a basic element within the overarching function of a manager. No two ways about it. Simple as that.

5. **Approachable** (note: there is a difference between being available and approachable; and approachable is infact a pre-requisite for being a reasonably good listener (the first pointer). Kinda ties-in together. You can't have one or the other. Got to have both.

However, I will say this; a manager needs to have the desired people skills to better understand and read into his/her team-members.

He / She certainly cannot afford to lead based on perceptions, but with more objectivity & empathy.

I find Jacinda Arden as that leader who in recent times is one of the very few personalities who has displayed utmost empathy and has ably managed to keep her constituents largely unaffected by the pandemic (reports suggest that not more than 25 deaths were recorded nationwide due to COVID.)

She has been praised for her compassion in handling anti-immigrant hate crimes that claimed about 50 lives by thumbing it down decisively in the bud, and her effectiveness in managing another tragedy of volcanic explosion that claimed 21 lives is worthy of a mention. She has demonstrated **responsiveness** and has shown **fairness** to the causes of concern.

Jacinda is the 40th PM of New Zealand and a youngest to serve the premiership at the age of 37.

She has emerged as a beacon of hope and a leader to look upto in today's world order.

I would think that Jacinda is the manager one would want!

Before this book went into publication, I heard yesterday that Jacinda Arden has announced her resignation from the PMs post voluntarily and has been praised for doing so for the reasons she mentioned.

One more strong reason why I think she is a better manager. Knowing when to call it off is a rare trait that a leader can possess in today's world.

Jacinda was quoted as below:

"I am not leaving because it was hard," Ardern said. "Had that been the case I probably would have departed two months into the job. I am leaving because with such a privileged role, comes responsibility, the responsibility to know when you are the right person to lead, and also when you are not."

8 ARE YOU WORKING FOR A BRAND?

Building a brand is more than raking in accounts, higher EBITDA, flashing big flex boards on a highway, or establishing a logo, nor is it about CSR activities that gets prime space in company websites & annual reports; and definitely not *just* customer-centricity. It's more than this. It's a combination of factors and it starts from **'within'**.

Brand building is ensuring that both internal and external stakeholders aren't treated any less and both get UNEQUIVOCAL focus across seasons!

This key trait sets your organization apart, and possibly gets you on the 'admired list' too! (Makes the organization a Leader in its own right.)

Here's a list of 10 factors that possibly would aid in building an inclusive & brand-worthy organization:

1. **Quality** (emphasis is to prioritize on 'quality outcome' than volume business)

Ensure the **Quality** credo is non-negotiable at your workplace.

Quality as I understand is a way-of-life (sounds philosophical? perhaps it is, but true.)

> It applies to every aspect of our day-to-day life.
>
> It is a continuous process.
>
> It is consistency – 'starting from the messages that one puts-out to the execution of the same'.
>
> Quality is doing the right thing always! (can't overstate this enough.)

Quality has no single definition, but I believe it should be the single most unambiguous goal for every initiative/project or program. Over here, the means are as important as the end, which I believe at times is compromised a whole lot.

I truly liked the example of the airplane readiness that I happened read somewhere, where the airplane is tested/confirmed for its flight prior to its take-off and there is no-scope whatsoever to tinker around the mechanisms during fly-time. We should adopt this approach to every process & product across the industry and across seasons. Be it in drug development, fintech, system-engineering, auto design & development etc.

Quality ought to be omnipresent, but the truth of the matter is: 'it is given a pass in majority of the scenarios unless made to comply with.'

2. Character & Culture

Totally depends on how strongly your Ethical Practices are followed in dealing with employees and clients alike. Treat both on par. Your reputation is driven largely from within. It would be callous to ignore internal stakeholders who are your real brand ambassadors.

3. Caring

What are the programs you have put in-place to ensure employee well-being in the truest sense - don't say we have ATM facility onsite, covered car parking etc., but ensure you have programs such as:

a crèche onsite, counselling services, fool proof 'retaliation' policies, unambiguous HR policies etc.

4. Approachability

Anybody should be able to talk/question anybody across the hierarchy without any fear or favor.

5. Inclusiveness

Take everyone along - '**Antyodaya**' (serve the last man in the line.)

6. Advertising

Get back to basics! Define yourself - think real on 'why you are doing what you are doing'?

7. Customer Service

Don't cut corners, be honest, be flexible, be nimble, apply the principle of 'good enough proceed on' and ask for **accountability from your customer** - it isn't taboo to ask that, no matter how small you are. Genuity & Diligence will fetch dividends and is long-term, which truly stays.

8. Social Responsibility programs

Look within - "charity begins from home". It would be a classic blunder if you cut down on the medical insurance of your employees but would sponsor a 'walk or run' on environmental awareness. That's just ***silly.*** Junk those practices!

9. Clear Vision

Educate employees on the vision.

Break it down. Try and explain how the ***company*** vision translates to ***department*** vision and how it eventually percolates to the ***project-level*** and aids the ***day-to-day mission***.

Why? Simply, because the larger population is clueless on how the vision ties-up with the day-to-day mission.

Breaking down vision to the detail and linking it to the ground-level executions while also retaining the big-picture helps in a number of ways and this value-add cannot be undermined because it not only enhances productivity but can eliminate 2 fundamental problems:

Any **commotion in delivery** and

Less than **basic understanding of the demand**

You will need leaders (change agents) at all levels who come with enough clarity and a sense of big-picture to take up this arduous task of educating people on vision.

10. Roll out unambiguous RACI chart (Organization wide!)

This has deeper impact (+ve) and rewards' handsomely!

Clarity in 'roles and responsibilities' is lacking in many of the established and highly acclaimed, *metrics-driven* and *process-oriented* entities, which is why it shouldn't be a surprise when you hear of greater than expected **attrition** (especially in mid-level and above role), so a clear RACI should help here.

I have come to believe that true 'employee engagement' **broadly** rests on the above 10 pointers. No-doubt they are loaded statements; got to address a lot of variants to get to the desired state.

These factors would lead to building a **culture** that helps the *scalable quotient for the* *organization to thrive.* It could be openness, **accepting of ideas, encouraging innovation**, being accessible & available etc.

Also, it's a no-brainer that an engaged work force drives **productivity, efficiency** and leads to **excellence in delivery** where enhanced **quality** is very much integral. All this aids the cause.

We are told time & again that businesses are all about the money (the bottom line), but I believe it's a little more than money that makes you a "BRAND". You got to honor innovation, appreciate true value-addition, recognize & reward talent/merit, call out false aspects, demonstrate leadership and build a rock-solid foundation with no-bias practices.

The above combination of factors when put in-place sets the organization apart from any type of competition. You will for sure have repeat customers and new revenues aren't hard to come!

When I was moving from the US back to India in 2011, I had to sell both my cars. I sold my first car – acura integra 2 door hatchback – pretty quick even though my wife was reluctant to let go. That car was with us since we started together, travelled all over, and had some fun memories. I however, held on to my 2nd car – 5 series BMW – for a few months only to finalize the sale a few days before we boarded and made our onward journey to Namma

Bengaluru!

Why am I talking about my move and the cars? Because when I had put up my BMW for sale, I met a lot of interested folks, one of whom was a guy who worked for Google. I remembered from our small talk back then, which may resonate with the topic of discussion in this chapter that Google builds & configures each laptop from scratch to be used by their personnel/new hires, thereby eliminating buying from other vendors. As per him, this is how Google ensures to provide the best powered machines to its employees, while this indigenous approach to build their own laptops no-doubt helps the company better address their inventory, logistical challenges, services & support.

I remember my buyer also mentioned that Google is a flat organization, with a lot less hierarchy across employee levels. The is one other trait that sets the organization apart – ties back to approachability.

Not sure, how much any of this is true though.

I, however, felt compelled to mention this story because I find it quite relevant to many of the elements mentioned in this chapter that makes a Brand.

And I am to understand (based on the data available in public domain) that Google provides the best benefits that a company can offer to its personnel, demonstrating the caring component.

I believe Google is the leader and the brand that many would want to be associated with.

9 HALO EFFECT AND LEADERSHIP CRISIS

Most would argue that any Industry segment most-certainly needs to have leaders who are known for their technical competency or hands-on technical skills; then where is the question of Halo effect when this is the expected norm?

However, its beyond doubt that any type of Industry needs managerial prowess to build a sustainable and scalable organization.

Managerial abilities can strategically and tactically handle economic, political, social, technological (PEST) factors while not ignoring the key foresight to 'Identify and Address' business opportunities and a market demand that will help scale a product, which *only* technicalities or technical controls cannot accomplish.

"Technology as such provides no value-addition if it isn't for the business demand". We have many more examples of failed initiatives for the lack of foresight, lack of business driver and not knowing how to navigate PEST factors.

Technical Expertise + Managerial Acumen + Product Vision is an unbeatable stack of traits, though. But that's a rarity, isn't it? The topic of discussion here is limited to 'hands-on technologists who are pushed or promoted to leadership roles.

In one of the earlier chapters, I reflected upon 2 broad categories of leaders (one who holds a position of authority; the other who inspires and drives by eliciting a sense of purpose.)

Of the 2 broad categories of leaders, the one who holds a position of authority and just goes about the day-to-day mechanics without instilling any passion is more often a result of the ***'Halo Effect'*** is what I think. This is a pitfall that many organizations of varying sizes have no doubt experienced and most certainly have paid heavily when realized.

Technical Competency **alone** is most often mis-understood for Managerial virtues. I am being modest here given the many cases that are widely prevalent to this day, Sad!

Folks who have moved into leadership roles **only** because of their technical competency find themselves clueless or rather helpless when faced with process related challenges, compliance/regulations, audit cycles, implementing a robust delivery-structure and more importantly when faced with a herculean task ***to build a scalable and sustainable world-class organization*** (the one which actually delivers while complying with the industry standards and best-practices; because more often, delivery is considered as an end-goal, but it seems to be a forgotten learning that ***'Best Practices imbibed into Delivery'*** is what makes the results stand-out and helps build a truly class-apart organization.

Halo-Effect leaders would relate **less** to establishing the very fabric that helps build an ***inclusive organization*** and that is (to name a few):

- talent-recognition
- imbibing a culture
- retention
- reward
- respect!

Inclusive initiatives such as building an ecosystem for growth and treating individuals the same way that you want to be treated should be **non-negotiable** (believe me, this needs more work and character by the leader.)

These no-doubt remains in the dossier of any organization, which is never seriously looked-into but only when scorched.

10 LEARNINGS FROM LEADERS

What good is a leader if there are zero traits or behavioral skills that one can pick up from? A leader who can inspire folks across the spectrum (within an organization or outside) will only create assets and add value along the way. This marks true respect and builds credibility for the leader.

I had the fortune to learn a few good practices from my leaders both in the past and present. In fact, I have always unknowingly looked out for something that stands out in my leaders. I have to say that this desire to learn and to be awed in a way has more or less hit a 50-50 ratio in my career, which I believe is pretty outstanding because note that, not all who hold a position of authority is a leader and hence cannot be held captive to this in-tangible quality.

I consulted for a big biopharma a few years ago and my leader who had hired me into his group informed us of his planned exit a few months down the lane. He had put down his papers, his last-working day was nearing (~10 days or so), his replacement was finalized, and the transition was closing in. We (his reporting team) were focusing on the day-to-day operations and other projects in our group. No-doubt the enterprise solution and its adjacencies that my leader was accountable for, had its own share of deliberations and success, which certainly was a thing to manage in the overly active environment with varying demands from customers across the globe.

With my leader's last day at work nearing; I was hoping that he would take it easy. But, to my surprise I only saw him sticking out till the last day, managing the over-whelming demands with actively engaging the user-community, participating/hosting meetings, driving resolutions in a cross-functional group and keeping himself on top of every nuance to the last minute.

I did ask him why since he any-ways had his directs taking-care of the day-to-day functions. He responded by saying that he would continue to function as usual to the very last day and treat it as any other day on the job. That is something which has always stayed with me, and I have tried my best to follow suit in the many consulting gigs that I have had since then.

Pretty hard to follow when you know your current role has turned into a mere customary option and more importantly when most in the organization would already know of the exit and to add to that, folks may not take you seriously given your short availability. But, despite that, this leader ensured that it was business as usual till his last working day.

Similarly, I have had other experiences where I have learnt to be grateful, to listen, to show up, to remain grounded (even when in a position of authority, which is needed more than ever, right?)

ABOUT THE AUTHOR

Pradeep is an independent consultant for the Pharma & Healthcare Industry with 20 years of vast experience in implementing tech and process controls across markets. He is an amateur investor too.

REFERENCES

Larry Ellison – All or Nothing – https://thenewsmen.co.in/high-flyers/ma-huateng-meet-the-ceo-and-co-founder-of-tencent/94768

https://www.cnbc.com/2017/09/11/10-billionaires-who-grew-up-dirt-poor.html

Jay Z – The Power to Choose – https://www.usmagazine.com/celebrity-news/news/jay-z-sold-crack-as-a-teenager-i-was-thinking-about-surviving-2013110/

https://digitalmag.theceomagazine.com/us/august-21/inspire/jay-z/

https://www.britannica.com/biography/Jay-Z

Howard Schultz – Take me to your Leader –

https://stories.starbucks.com/leadership/howard-schultz/

https://www.masterclass.com/articles/howard-schultz-life-and-career

https://www.forbes.com/profile/howard-schultz/?sh=e18732352c64

https://www.businessinsider.in/2-brilliant-management-strategies-howard-schultz-used-to-build-the-starbucks-coffee-empire/articleshow/51245934.cms

Luis Urzua – No-Non Sense Leader

https://www.cbsnews.com/news/chilean-miners-leadership-lessons-from-luis-urzua/

https://www.britannica.com/event/Chile-mine-rescue-of-2010

Jacinda Arden NZ PM – What should you want in a Manager?
https://www.britannica.com/biography/Jacinda-Ardern/The-2017-election

https://www.usatoday.com/story/news/world/2023/01/19/new-zealand-prime-minister-jacinda-ardern-resigns/11080726002/

www.ingramcontent.com/pod-product-compliance
Lightning Source LLC
Chambersburg PA
CBHW071122240526
45465CB00022B/770